CLEOPATRA

A Life From Beginning to End

Copyright © 2017 by Hourly History.

All rights reserved.

Table of Contents

Introduction
The Ptolemaic Dynasty
Cleopatra as Queen
Cleopatra and Julius Caesar
Venus and Dionysus
Mark Antony and Cleopatra
Cleopatra's Empire
Antony and Cleopatra Reunited
Propaganda Wars
A War to End All Wars
The Last Pharaoh of Egypt
Conclusion

Introduction

"History is written by the victors," said Sir Winston Churchill. Cleopatra was not a victor and her history was written, in large part, by her enemies.

The Greek and Roman writers who documented Cleopatra's life and downfall in the century following her death were the heirs and beneficiaries of the men who destroyed her. We know a handful of incontrovertible facts known about Cleopatra—that she was Greek Macedonian, not Egyptian; that she deposed her brother to ascend to the throne of Egypt; that she had children with both Julius Caesar and Markus Antonius; and that she committed suicide—the rest is up for interpretation.

During Cleopatra's reign, Egyptians were highly literate, and Cleopatra likely wrote frequently during her life. The Romans who took Cleopatra's throne either destroyed these valuable primary materials or neglected them until they disappeared. Without a solid evidentiary foundation on which to build an accurate historical account of Cleopatra's life, writers from ancient times to modern day have made liberal use of their imagination.

To some, Cleopatra was a goddess. "The most complete woman to have ever existed, the most womanly woman and the most queenly queen," said Theophile Gautier. Cleopatra represented a serious threat to the status quo of the ancient world where powerful men invaded, conquered, and ruled. The only woman in all of classical antiquity to rule a kingdom independently, not as a successor but as an heir, and the last Pharaoh of Egypt, Cleopatra is a reMarkable historical figure. While ultimately defeated by the unstoppable expansion of the almighty Roman kingdom, during her reign Cleopatra proved herself as a talented diplomat, an accomplished naval commander, and a proficient administrator and linguist.

Yet to some, Cleopatra was nothing more than a seductress, an insignificant appendage to the powerful men she was involved with. "Cleopatra was of no moment whatsoever in the policy of Caesar the Dictator, but merely a brief chapter in his amours," said historian Ronald Syme. According to some, Cleopatra used her famous beauty to manipulate two great Roman figures into orchestrating their own downfall. She was a monstrous woman, both seductress and sorceress, and to serve her was a disgrace to men of Roman blood.

In reality, Cleopatra's position as the only independent queen of the Ptolemaic dynasty to rule successfully alone forced her to choose a male partner who would benefit her kingdom. For Cleopatra, romantic love would always go hand in hand with state policy. Regardless of who fathered her children, Cleopatra was a legendary queen. Speculation and innuendo will always obscure the details of Cleopatra's life, but by taking a journey through the time and place in which Cleopatra lived, we can at least catch a glimpse of the most powerful woman to rule the ancient world.

Chapter One

The Ptolemaic Dynasty

"Bury my body and don't build any monument. Keep my hands out so the people know the one who won the world had nothing in hand when he died."

—Alexander the Great

Little is known of Cleopatra's life before her fight for the Egyptian throne at age 19 or 20. But the conditions of her upbringing and political situation at the time offer an intriguing insight into the making of the future queen.

Cleopatra was born early in the year 69 BCE in Egypt's ancient capital, Alexandria, the daughter of Ptolemy XII Auletes. A clear and indisputable descendent of a long line of Ptolemaic kings, Ptolemy XII was descended from Alexander the Great's general, Ptolemy I. Cleopatra was the second of five children, and although we know the identity of Cleopatra's siblings, the identity of her mother is unknown. Cleopatra's siblings—Berenike IV, Ptolemy XIII, Ptolemy XIV, and Arsinoe IV—may have been borne by two different women. It is likely that Cleopatra's mother was Cleopatra VI of Egypt, both sister and wife of Ptolemy XII, but there is speculation that Cleopatra's mother was Ptolemy XII's second wife, an unknown member of the Egyptian priestly family of Ptah.

Ptolemy XII was born at the end of the second century BCE, heir to the throne of a country that was reaching a crisis point. Roman interference in Egyptian politics was becoming threatening, and the Ptolemaic Empire was crumbling from within. As was common in the Ptolemaic dynasty, a violent sibling struggle preceded Ptolemy XII's ascension to the throne. Indicative of the patriarchal society of the time, Ptolemy XII's sister Cleopatra Berenike III was direct heir but opposition to her ruling alone was so strong that she was forced to marry Ptolemy XI, her own stepson. Ptolemy XI killed Cleopatra Berenike III, and the people of Egypt killed Ptolemy XI in the ensuing riot. Into this bloody quagmire of family politics stepped King Ptolemy XII.

Unsurprisingly, the murderous antics of the Ptolemaic dynasty had given them a bad reputation amongst the Egyptian people. Powerful factions in Alexandria routinely questioned Ptolemy XII's claim to the throne, casting aspersions on his ancestry. The threat of Rome also loomed large, as Ptolemy X, Ptolemy XII's father, had willed Egypt to the Romans as collateral for loans he never repaid. Rome could conceivably lay claim to Egypt at any time.

At the same time that disenfranchised native Egyptians were tiring of the absolute monarchy of the Ptolemaic dynasty and its mediocre leadership, Rome was becoming the strongest political power in the Mediterranean. Rome had conquered most of Greece by the second century BCE, and Ptolemy XII's Egypt existed in its shadow, an independent nation on paper but one that was essentially dependent on Rome for its freedom.

When Cleopatra was ten, her father made the disastrous move of debasing the country's coinage and then exacting a huge tax rise, causing a keenly felt economic depression that led to rebellion. Ptolemy XII turned to Rome for help with his domestic problems. With the backing of one of the three most powerful Roman leaders—politician Julius Caesar, General Gnaeus Pompeius, and businessman Markus Crassus—Ptolemy believed that he could force his subjects to respect him. In 59 BCE, he used the already diminished Egyptian treasury to pay Caesar a huge sum of money in exchange for confirming him as a friend and ally of Rome and possibly a Roman citizen. Soon after, Rome annexed Ptolemaic-ruled Cyprus and Ptolemy did nothing. In response, his subjects again rebelled and forced Ptolemy XII to flee to Rome.

It is impossible to know how much Cleopatra understood the instability of the kingdom she would one day rule. Cleopatra spent her childhood with her sisters, insulated within one of the most refined and luxurious palaces of the ancient world. Cleopatra was raised in Alexandria, the largest, most cosmopolitan and learned cities in the world. Part of the Ptolemaic palace complex, the famous Great Library of Alexandria and its sister museum offered their most gifted scholars to tutor Cleopatra. According to Plutarch, who wrote a biography of Mark Antony, the future queen spoke Syrian, Arabic, Hebrew, Greek, and Egyptian with fluency. For the children of King Ptolemy XII, Alexandria was a splendid and enchanting playground that shaped the future rulers into adults who were educated, worldly, and decadent in the extreme.

When Ptolemy XII entered self-exile in 58 BCE, his sister and former wife, Cleopatra VI, emerged from obscurity to snatch the throne. Berenike, the eldest daughter of Cleopatra VI and Ptolemy, also made a claim for the throne, and it is thought that this mother-daughter duo of queens took the unusual step of ruling in tandem for a time. Cleopatra VI died under suspicious circumstances in the year 55 BCE, not long before Ptolemy returned to Egypt. Meanwhile, Berenike spent time choosing the husband that would legitimize her rule.

Berenike and her husband, Archelaos, were poised to rule Egypt independently, a situation that did not sit well with Rome. Ptolemy XII convinced Gabinius, the governor of Syria, to invade Egypt and restore him to his throne. The invasion was a success. King Archelaos was killed in battle, and Berenike III was executed alongside many of her wealthiest supporters.

One of the young Roman officers to invade Egypt at this time was Mark Antony. A cavalry commander in his first provincial post, Antony kept a close eye on the political events unfolding around him. When Antony was welcomed to the Ptolemaic palace, Cleopatra was 14 years old and could not have escaped intimate knowledge of her father's exile, her stepmother's strange death, and sister's execution. At the time these future lovers met, they were each being shaped by the chronic instability they were living through. Later in his life, Antony admitted that he fell in love with Cleopatra at first sight.

It is a surprise to most to learn that Cleopatra was not in fact Egyptian. Cleopatra was born into a dynasty of Macedonian Greek heritage and was, at most, one-quarter Egyptian on her mother's side. When Cleopatra inherited Egypt, it was a deeply divided country, segregated along the lines of class and race. The rise of the Ptolemaic dynasty had attracted Greeks to Egypt, but these new immigrants did not mix with native Egyptians and viewed themselves as a superior race. ReMarkably quickly, Greek became the lingua franca of Egypt and prejudice against native Egyptians was rife. Cleopatra's mixed ancestry became important once she became queen as her ability to speak both the Egyptian and Greek language and her deep knowledge of Egyptian culture, history, and customs won her the love and respect of her people.

Chapter Two

Cleopatra as Queen

"Since there seemed to be no other way of getting in, she stretched herself out at full length inside a sleeping bag, and Apoodorus, after tying up the bag, carried it indoors to Caesar."

—Plutarch

As soon as Gabinius restored Ptolemy XII to his throne, the king wrote his will. As Cleopatra was the only child of his nearing adulthood (his oldest son Ptolemy XIII was eight years old), and she was the obvious heir to his throne. But in his will, Ptolemy listed both Cleopatra and his son, Ptolemy XIII, as joint heir. He also listed "the Roman people" as guardians of the future king and queen. This line was unusual and was perhaps included to provide a legal loophole for future Roman interference in Egypt.

In the spring of 52 BCE, Cleopatra became joint regent with her father, a position that brought her little power but bestowed upon her the title of "new god." Ptolemy XII also gave this title to his son, Ptolemy XIII, in the vain hope that these siblings would harmoniously share power. On Ptolemy XII's death in early 51 BCE, both siblings ascended to the throne, but Cleopatra immediately made it clear that she did not intend to share her throne with her younger brother.

Cleopatra asserted herself in the following months by stepping out into the public eye and making the 400-mile trip up the Nile to attend a sacred Buchis bull ceremony as queen. She also removed her brother's name from official court documents. The kingdom Cleopatra was fighting to rule was racked by civil strife, crippled by outstanding debt to Rome and destabilized by corrupt public officials. In the year 48 BCE Egypt's difficulties were expounded by a major drought and subsequent famine.

Soon Cleopatra's brother, who had not yet reached his teens, was proving to be a serious rival for the throne. A band of powerful advisors surrounded the boy, including his tutor and legal administrator Potheinos, and plotted ways to rid Egypt of its queen. Despite, or perhaps by necessity of, these trying conditions, Cleopatra devoted herself to creating an easy diplomacy with Rome and a mutually respectful relationship with her subjects.

The ruling siblings were able to present a united front in the summer of 49 BCE. Gnaeus, the son of Pompeius the Great, arrived in Alexandria to request military assistance against Julius Caesar. The rivalry between Pompeius and Caesar had been simmering for two decades and had finally reached a breaking point when Caesar broke his exile and returned to Italy, forcing Pompeius to withdraw to Greece.

Cleopatra and her brother gifted Pompeius 60 ships and 500 troops, reinforcements that did not ultimately lead Pompeius to victory but did repay a measure of the outstanding debts the siblings had inherited from their father. Shortly after this successful diplomatic move, Cleopatra found herself forced to leave Alexandria. Ptolemy's advisors had upped their game, and it seemed that her life was in danger. Rather than retreating quietly into a place of refuge, Cleopatra went to Syria where she set about building an army.

Establishing herself in Antioch where she had family connections, Cleopatra sought support from the rulers of Askalon and fueled opposition to Pompeius whom she now saw as having betrayed her. As spring of 48 BCE turned into summer, events in Greece were working in Cleopatra's favor. Pompeian and Caesarian forces clashed at Pharsalus in August, and the defeat suffered by Pompeius' troops could not have been more absolute. With his trusty and talented General Antony at his side, Caesar led his troops to slaughter 15,000 Pompeians and capture a further 24,000.

Pompeius escaped with his life but was forced to seek sanctuary in Egypt where he hoped Ptolemy XIII would respect his historic bond with the Ptolemaic dynasty and assist him. Whether the boy king intended to protect Pompeius or not is hard to discern as Ptolemy's advisors swiftly took control and laid a trap for Pompeius. Either the advisors were naively hoping to keep Egypt out of the Roman civil war or they were callously choosing Caesar's side in the dispute. Whatever their motives, Ptolemy's advisors accepted Pompeius' request for safe passage but when he arrived in Alexandria and tried to disembark from his ship he was beheaded.

Believing that offering proof of Pompeius' death would please Caesar, Ptolemy had Pompeius' severed head delivered to Caesar on his arrival at the royal palace in Alexandria. Caesar was disgusted. Taking on both Pompeius' historic friendship with the Ptolemaic dynasty and the outstanding debts owed to him by Egypt, Caesar strongly suggested that Ptolemy and Cleopatra settle their differences and pay him a portion of the 17.5 million drachmas Egypt owed Rome in the meantime.

Cleopatra now orchestrated one of the most famous encounters of her life. Cleopatra knew that she had to win Caesar's favor if she was ever going to rule Egypt alone and so arranged to meet with him in secret. In the most entertaining account of this meeting, provided by Plutarch, Cleopatra had herself tied up in a bed sack and smuggled into Caesar's rooms. Once Cleopatra was stood before Caesar dressed in all her regal finery, it didn't take long for him to be charmed to take her side.

Caesar called Cleopatra and Ptolemy to a meeting of the Alexandrian Assembly where he read and promised to enforce the particulars of Ptolemy XII's will. In addition to naming Cleopatra and Ptolemy as joint rulers in the Egyptian tradition, Caesar bestowed Cyprus upon the younger Ptolemaic siblings, Arsinoe and Ptolemy XIV. Sending Cleopatra's siblings, who were still pre-adolescents, far away from Egypt was a gift to Cleopatra, but none of these arrangements would ever happen. Ptolemy's powerful advisors were not content to share power with Cleopatra and rebelled, giving orders for the Egyptian army to attack Caesar.

What became known as the Alexandrian War lasted the rest of 48 BCE and early 47 BCE. The most famous casualty of this conflict was not a person but an institution, the Library of Alexandria. Historians regard the burning of entire collections of ancient Alexandrian documents as one of the greatest disasters of antiquity.

Arsinoe, Cleopatra's younger sister, came into prominence during the Alexandrian War, at one point raising an army and having herself declared queen. When Arsinoe and Ptolemy XIII joined forces, it seemed Caesar would soon be defeated, but reinforcements from Asia and Askalon arrived just in time. The last battle of the Alexandrian War was fought in early 47 BCE. Ptolemy XIII was killed in battle, and Arsinoe was captured and sent into exile. Throughout this period, Cleopatra lived in quiet seclusion within the royal palace at Alexandria waiting for news from the frontlines. That Ptolemy XIII and his most powerful advisors had been eliminated was certainly good news for Cleopatra, but she was harboring glad tidings of her own—the queen of Egypt was pregnant.

Chapter Three

Cleopatra and Julius Caesar

"The fault, dear Brutus, is not in our stars but in ourselves."

—William Shakespeare, Julius Caesar

If Plutarch's account is to be believed then Cleopatra and Caesar were so taken with each other after their first meeting in the palace that they quickly became lovers. Cleopatra was 21 years old at the time and Caesar 52. According to Plutarch, Cleopatra captivated Caesar with her "provocative impudence" and, as Caesar was no stranger to sexual liaisons with powerful women, an affair seemed inevitable.

Cleopatra's interest in Caesar may have been strictly political. Caesar had the power to destroy Cleopatra's brother and rival, and Cleopatra knew she needed him on her side. That said, Caesar was a bold and brave leader, a vain man who was an accomplished politician and a learned scholar. It is entirely within the realms of possibility that Cleopatra and Caesar were mutually attracted to each other and that the pair developed a true bond.

When Caesar had Cleopatra officially reinstated as the queen of Egypt, it is likely that he knew she was pregnant with his child. That Cleopatra's child belonged to Caesar predictably became a charged political issue in later years, when rivals questioned the child's parentage and suitability to succeed Cleopatra's throne. For now, however, Cleopatra's pregnancy seemed irrelevant. As part of the ceremony reinstating Cleopatra as queen, she was married to her 12-year-old brother Ptolemy XIV. The marriage of royal siblings was a long-standing Egyptian tradition, and Caesar's insistence that the union take place was a calculated political move. The 12-year-old boy had no advisors and no political power, but his presence as a joint ruler satisfied critics of a female-led monarchy. Cleopatra was finally free to rule alone.

To show Caesar her appreciation, Cleopatra organized a long river cruise up the Nile. Sources written after the fact report that more than 400 ships took part in this decadent procession and that Cleopatra and Caesar spent these months as lovers. By the spring of 47 BCE, Caesar was forced to leave Egypt and return to Italy to finally finish the civil war he had begun. At this time, Cleopatra was also nearing the end of her pregnancy. With Caesar's wife, the respected Roman noblewoman Calpurnia, back in Rome, Caesar perhaps saw it as prudent to distance himself from Cleopatra.

Cleopatra gave birth on June 23, 47 BCE. In an attempt to quell any suspicions about the child's parentage, Cleopatra had her son christened with the official name Pharaoh Caesar, the dynastic name Ptolemy XV, and the given name Caesarion. It is difficult to untangle Caesar's attitude towards his new son. Caesar's marriage of over ten years to Calpurnia was childless, and when he returned to Rome, news of his fruitful liaison with Cleopatra made him public enemy number one. It seems that Caesar denied being the father of Caesarion in public, making no mention of the child in his will, but admitted it in private and allowed Cleopatra to keep his name.

At the time of Caesarion's birth, Caesar was in Asia fighting Pharnakes, son of Mithradates the Great. Once Caesar had secured victory, he returned to Rome to celebrate a string of significant military victories. Caesar invited Cleopatra to Rome with her brother and husband, the young Ptolemy XIV, to take part in his great triumphal display. It is not clear whether Cleopatra took her infant son with her to Rome, but it would have been sensible to do so, both to protect her child and show the Roman people his resemblance to Caesar.

Caesar housed the royal couple in his magnificent villa on the river Tiber, a move that insulated the queen from undesired contact with the Roman Senate. Cleopatra was treated as the most distinguished guest ever to grace the city of Rome and received a string of notable visitors. Among these visitors was Cicero, a former consul and powerful politician who took a strong and instant dislike to Cleopatra.

In September 46 BCE, Caesar dedicated the Forum Julium with its Temple of Venus Genetrix to Cleopatra and had a golden statue made in her likeness placed in the precinct. This act drew clear parallels between Cleopatra and Venus, the mother of the Roman people, and

Cleopatra and Isis, the goddess most associated with Ptolemaic Egypt. Cleopatra also influenced Caesar in his plans to build the first public library in Rome and his preparations for an Alexandrian calendar reform. Cicero and his fellow senators regarded these developments with distaste and feared that Caesar might overthrow the Senate and turn Rome into a dictatorship.

Despite the antagonistic relationship between Cicero and Caesar, the former consul was as shocked as anybody when Caesar was assassinated on Markh 15, 44 BCE. Three members of the Roman Senate, Cassius Longuis, Decimus Brutus, and Markus Brutus, whipped daggers out from beneath their robes and stabbed Caesar to death in the Senate House. Cleopatra was either still residing in Rome at the time of Caesar's murder or had returned for a second time. When she heard the horrifying news, she gathered her belongings and left for Egypt immediately.

Cleopatra arrived back in Alexandria in July 44 BCE where she mourned the death of Caesar while keeping a close eye on political developments back in Rome. Caesar was an incredibly powerful man, and his assassination left a power vacuum that resulted in two years of political and military upheaval. In 43 BCE, Antony, who was Caesar's next in line as consul at the time of his murder, Octavian, Caesar's 18-year-old adopted son, and Lepidus, a powerful general, constituted a political triumvirate that was to last five years.

Ostensibly, these three men united in order to restore the Roman Republic and bring law and order back to the disrupted Roman realm. In reality, the men engaged in a brutal purge of all of their political enemies, even murdering Cicero in cold blood. Once they had eliminated their enemies at home, the triumvirate turned its attention to Caesar's assassins, who had fled to Greece to raise troops. A devastating confrontation between Rome's two most powerful military factions was looming, and Cleopatra was about to be forced to choose sides.

Chapter Four

Venus and Dionysus

"The word spread on every side that Venus had come to revel with Dionysus."

—Plutarch

Cassius, one of Caesar's assassins sent out a request for soldiers and economic aid to the rulers of kingdoms in the Near East, including Cleopatra. When Caesar left Egypt following his romantic cruise up the River Nile with Cleopatra, he left four legions of Roman soldiers behind; it was these four legions that Cassius had his eye on. But Cleopatra decided that the situation in Egypt was too unstable for her to spare the troops and sent the four legions to Proconsul Dolabella of Syria, a Caesarian loyalist, instead.

Cleopatra was no longer neutral. When Cassius intercepted Cleopatra's four legions of troops heading for Syria, it became clear that Cleopatra would have to make her allegiance to the triumvirate known and negotiate for their protection should Cassius try to invade Egypt.

As Cassius' army grew, Cleopatra provisioned her own fleet and took on the role of naval commander, leading her fleet's journey to the west coast of Greece where she intended to assist Antony and Octavian. Riding the waves like a human incarnation of the divine Isis, Cleopatra's readiness to go into battle was rare among queens of the time and cemented her image as a goddess among men.

Cassius sent his fleet of ships to the Greek coast with the intention of cutting Cleopatra off, but the two forces never engaged. Cleopatra's fleet was badly damaged in a storm, and Cleopatra herself was absent from fulfilling her naval commander duties because she was ill with seasickness the entire time she as at sea. Still, the intention was there, and in return for her nautical adventure, Cleopatra demanded that the triumvirate recognize Caesarion as Caesar's son, which they did.

Cleopatra receded from the civil war at this point and returned to manage her kingdom at Alexandria. Shrewd enough to know that she needed to stay well informed on developments in the ongoing civil war, Cleopatra left secret agents behind in Greece. In the fall of 42 BCE the civil war reached its climax at the Battle of Philippi. The armies fought two pitched battles three weeks apart. The battles were long and brutal, and by the end of the second battle Brutus and Cassius's army was completely destroyed. Defeated, Brutus and Cassius committed suicide, and with their deaths, any hope for the restoration of a true Roman Republic died too.

With the civil war over, the triumvirate set about dividing Rome between them. Lepidus received only the Roman provinces of North Africa. Octavian took the west, including Spain and the large island of Sardinia, and Antony took the east, including Roman provinces in Greece, Asia Minor, and the Near East. Antony had clearly emerged as the dominant member of the triumvirate. Antony's position as the master of the east also gave him huge authority over independent eastern kingdoms, including Egypt. It was only a matter of time before Antony and Cleopatra would meet.

Antony sent letters to Cleopatra, requesting her presence at his headquarters at Tarsos, which she duly ignored. It was arrogance on the part of Antony, a mere Roman magistrate to demand that Cleopatra leave her kingdom at his disposal. Eventually, convinced by a visit from Antony's most trusted aide, Q. Dellius, Cleopatra made the journey. It seemed Antony intended to quiz the young queen on her rumored support of Cassius during the last Roman civil war, but Cleopatra used the trip to her own ends, easily making Antony her sworn ally.

Cleopatra's approach to Tarsos up the Kydnos River is one of the most famous events of antiquity. A description, again written by Plutarch, insists that Cleopatra was dressed as the goddess Venus. Reclined on her barge beneath a canopy of gold cloth, Cleopatra surrounded herself with her most beautiful waiting-women, themselves dressed as minor goddesses. The procession of the barge was accompanied by mesmerizing flute music, and with each row of the barge's oars, wafts of sweet perfume were released into the air.

Cleopatra had set out to make an impression, and her entrance to Tarsos did not disappoint. Local people followed the procession from the riverbanks and Antony greeted the queen outside his headquarters. Cleopatra's choice of outfit was telling. In dressing as the goddess

Venus, Cleopatra was boldly allying herself on both a political and personal level with Antony, who identified himself as the human incarnation of the god Dionysus.

That night, Venus and Dionysus dined together on Cleopatra's barge along with a number of Antony's officers. Cleopatra's barge was decorated with rich tapestries and fine furniture, all lit by hundreds of oil lamps and wood-burning braziers. The effect was spectacular. Dinner was as lavish and theatrical as can be imagined and the queen demonstrated her generosity by allowing her many guests to take whatever furnishings they desired home with them.

The next night it was Antony's turn to host, and he joked easily about the embarrassing simplicity of his offering when compared to the decadence of the night before. Cleopatra showed how easily she could shift her countenance to suit her company and slipped into the relaxed, straight-talking manner Antony preferred. On the fourth day, Cleopatra again entertained on her barge, inviting her guests into a dining room filled with rose bouquets. The pleasantries dealt with, it was now time to talk business.

Antony confronted Cleopatra with his charge that she had aided Cassius during the civil war which she easily deflected by insisting that she had sent Caesar's Roman troops to Dolabella in Syria and led her fleet to Greece. Both of these attempts to help Antony had been unsuccessful and, as Dolabella had committed suicide, there was no real way to know what Cleopatra's motives were.

But Cleopatra's word was enough, for now, and having convinced Antony that she had his victory in mind, Cleopatra moved on to her second motive for this trip. Cleopatra needed Antony's help to eliminate the last two rivals for her throne. Cleopatra's sister, Arsinoe, had Markhed in chains during Caesar's triumph in Rome and held prisoner ever since within the Temple of Artemis in Ephesus. Despite Arsinoe's isolation from Egypt, a faction of Egyptians still supported her and recognized her as their true queen. Almost immediately, Arsinoe received a visit from one of Antony's assassins who dragged Arsinoe from the temple to her death.

Next, Cleopatra asked Antony to kill a second rival claiming to be Ptolemy XIII. Ptolemy, Cleopatra's brother and first husband, was supposedly killed in battle at the end of the Alexandrian War, but it was entirely possible that his supporters had faked his death and whisked him away to a quiet sanctuary from which they could build a new army. This threat, whether legitimate or not, had to be eliminated and Antony took care of it. Now, with no clear rival for her throne, Cleopatra was on her way to becoming the most powerful independent ruler in the east. Antony' assistance, however, was not an act of pure generosity. In return for Rome's protection against enemies, both domestic and foreign, Antony' asked Cleopatra to fund and assist him in his upcoming Parthian Campaign. Cleopatra agreed.

Chapter Five

Mark Antony and Cleopatra

"Come, sir, come,
I'll wrestle with you in my strength of love.
Look, here I have you, thus I let you go,
And give you to the gods."

—William Shakespeare, *Antony and Cleopatra*

With official business dealt with and a fondness for each other blossoming into a love affair, Cleopatra invited Antony to spend the winter with her in Alexandria. In November of 41 BCE, Antony arrived quietly in the Egyptian capital, cleverly neglecting to bring the legions of troops Caesar did on a similar visit. Antony did not appear as part of an army that threatened Egypt's independence; instead, he appeared and behaved as a highly distinguished guest of the queen.

Again, the splendor of life at the Alexandrian royal palace during Antony's visit is legendary and recounted in detail by Plutarch. Cleopatra threw parties where the guests drank and ate to excess, and she and Antony spent almost every day in each other's company. While it's entirely possible that Cleopatra had tender feelings for Antony, it's also important to consider Cleopatra's political motives for enjoying an affair with Antony.

As an independent queen who ruled her kingdom alone, Cleopatra VII was an anomaly. There had been unmarried queens in the Ptolemaic dynasty before. Cleopatra's aunt, Cleopatra Berenike III, and her sister, Berenike IV, reigned alone but both queens were pressured to marry and their reigns ended in their violent deaths. Effective female rulers can be found in earlier historical periods, such as Egyptian Queen Hatshepsut (fifteenth century BCE) and Halikarnassos Queen Artemisia (fifth century BCE), whom Cleopatra was likely influenced by. Subsequent queens such as Dynamis of Bosporos (17 BCE-7 CE) and Zenobia at Palmyra (267-72 CE) looked back to Cleopatra as their role model.

Cleopatra was blazing a trail for future independent queens, and to solidify her position and protect her kingdom she needed to produce another heir. Caesarion was growing well and Rome recognized him as Caesar's heir, but having just one heir was a precarious situation. Cleopatra did not seem to desire a husband or, if she did, no suitable candidate had yet appeared. Sibling marriage, the custom of the Ptolemaic dynasty, had not worked out for Cleopatra as both sibling-husbands had turned against her and neither union had produced an heir.

It is possible that early in her reign Cleopatra seriously looked for a husband from the Seleukid or Macedonian dynasties but now, around 28 or 29 years old, she had no desire to relinquish her power to a man. Yet the timing was fortuitous for Cleopatra to have another child. Ruling alone, Cleopatra had to take into account the stability of her kingdom and consider what factions may be waiting in the wings to usurp her before she became pregnant. The considerable health risk involved in giving birth to a child in Ancient Egypt also gave Cleopatra pause for thought, and in an attempt to limit the stress on her body she spaced her pregnancies out as much as she could. Caesarion was now seven years old.

Cleopatra knew that the kingdom of Egypt could only survive by allying itself with Rome. To create an heir with the most powerful Roman in the world was an obvious choice. Was Antony aware of Cleopatra's plans? Quite possibly. Antony was married to Fulvia, a prominent Roman woman who was deeply involved in the political machinations of Rome. Antony and Fulvia had two sons together and with Antony away at the court of Cleopatra for an entire winter, Fulvia must have expected what came next.

Antony and Cleopatra's long winter vacation came to an abrupt end in the spring of 40 BCE. A follower of Cassius' who had escaped the triumvirate's purge after Caesar's assassination, had raised an army and invaded Syria. Antony's new governor there, L. Decidius Saxa, had been murdered and his army seized. Antony had not planned his Parthian campaign to begin just yet but with the Parthian side seriously gaining strength, he was forced into action. The situation back in Italy had also grown unstable, and a rebellion against Octavian had gained pace, despite Antony's absence.

When Antony left to embark on his Parthian Campaign, Cleopatra was pregnant with twins. There is little to no record of Cleopatra's life once Antony left, and she probably receded from public life as her pregnancy advanced. There is no exact birth date for Cleopatra's twins but they arrived before the end of the year 40 BCE. Cleopatra named her children Cleopatra Selene and Alexander Helios, the sun and the moon. With Antony far away, leading his army, the children were not given surnames, but when Cleopatra and Antony finally met again in 37 BCE, Antony acknowledged his paternity of the children and allowed them to take the Antony name.

While Cleopatra was caring for her newborn twins in Alexandria, Antony was embarking on a new life as a newlywed. Much had occurred in Antony' life during Cleopatra's pregnancy. Antony's wife, Fulvia, had led a rebellion against Octavian known as the Perusine War that had failed so miserably that she was forced to flee to Greece. Antony's brother, Lucius, was also involved and was taken captive by Octavian. Fulvia died on her way to meet with Antony at Sikyon. It is not clear how Fulvia died or even whether her death was accidental, but the timing of Fulvia's death was incredibly fortuitous for Antony as it allowed him to reconcile with Octavian.

In a formal deal known as the Brundisium Agreement, Antony and Octavian again divided the Roman world between them with Antony in the east and Octavian in the west, the Ionian Sea forming a natural boundary. The Brundisium Agreement also included a marriage pact between the new allies. Now that Fulvia was dead, Antony was a widower and by chance, Octavian's sister, Octavia, had also recently lost her husband. Seen as a way to restore harmony to the Roman world, a familial marriage alliance between Octavian and Antony was very popular with the Roman people. How could Antony refuse?

Had Octavia been a woman who, like Antony's previous wives, was easily convinced to stay behind in Rome while Antony spent long periods in the presence of foreign queens, Cleopatra would not have needed to worry. As it was, Octavia was described as a "wonder of a woman" and was a clear rival for both Antony's affections and loyalty. Octavia gave birth to two children, both named Antonia, in 39 and 36 BCE. Both girls would go on to play a major role in the Roman world as the eldest Antonia was the grandmother of Emperor Nero and the youngest was the mother of Emperor Claudius.

Chapter Six

Cleopatra's Empire

*"All strange and terrible events are welcome,
But comforts we despise; our size of sorrow,
Proportion'd to our cause, must be as great."*

—William Shakespeare, *Antony and Cleopatra*

In the years following Antony's departure from Alexandria, Cleopatra focused her attention on ruling Egypt and expanding her territory abroad. When Cleopatra took the throne of Egypt, the Ptolemaic Empire was only a fraction of what it had once been. Caesar had returned Cyprus to Ptolemaic control at Cleopatra's request in 47 BCE, and now Cleopatra wanted control of Kilikia. Kilikia was a mountainous region of southern Asia Minor and home to the ancient city of Tarsos where Cleopatra and Antony held their famous meeting of minds. It is likely that Cleopatra first suggested that Antony return Kilikia to her during the meeting at Tarsos because by November 38 BCE, Kilikia was under Cleopatra's control.

In late 37 BCE, Antony and Cleopatra finally met again. Antony had cause to go east and orchestrate his war against the Parthians, and this time Octavia could not accompany him. With Octavia conveniently located in

Italy, Antony requested the presence of Cleopatra in Antioch, to which she obliged, bringing his three-year-old twins with her. If later accounts are to be believed, it was an emotional and passionate meeting, but once Antony and Cleopatra had made up for lost time they were forced to turn their attention to serious political matters.

A young Roman named Herod had become a threat to Egypt's stability. Herod was the son of Antipatros of Askalon, a former ally of Cleopatra's, and had appealed to Antony to give him a position in the southern Levant. Antony made Herod tetrarch (governor) of Judea, a notoriously unstable region. The Hasmonean family, who had ruled Judea for a century before Herod came along, would not recognize his rule and the region descended into civil war. Cleopatra had no wish to become embroiled in the events in Judea, and over the course of the civil war that lasted more than three years, she did not offer Herod assistance.

By late 37 BCE, Herod had managed to win the war and now posed a clear and present threat to Cleopatra's empire. Just before Antony met with Cleopatra, he had met with Octavian to renew the terms of the Brundisium Agreement. With Octavian's blessing, Antony had reorganized his territories in the east. It was beneficial to the Romans at this time to keep their Empire compact and to surround themselves with independent kingdoms and territories ruled by those friendly to Rome.

Antony completely redesigned the kingdoms of the eastern Mediterranean, creating new dynasties that took little notice of existing claimants to the throne. In all, five rulers took control of new territories. Galatia, the central section of Asia Minor was given to King Amyntas, a former Roman secretary. Kappadokia was given to King Archelaos, and the kingdom of Pontos in the north was given to King Polemon, both men with no royal or familial claim to the territory whatsoever. Herod was the fourth man enthroned by Antony and became the King of Judea. Finally, there was Queen Cleopatra, the only one of the five rulers who was the rightful dynastic heir to her throne, and, of course, the only woman.

Cleopatra benefited greatly from Antony's arrangements as he returned almost all of the Ptolemaic kingdom's former territory to her. Over the course of the next several years, Antony gave Cleopatra the Levantine coastal cities of Gaza, Ptolemais, and Byblos, and the coasts of Phoenicia and Palestine, all-important centers of trade. The most contentious gift Antony gave to Cleopatra was the city of Askalon, Herod's ancestral home in Judea. Even more irritating for Herod, Antony gave Cleopatra a particularly fertile tract of land close to the town of Jericho. This land was abundant with rich balsam-palm groves that were very valuable to Herod. Cleopatra agreed to lease the Judean land to King Herod for the significant sum of two hundred talents a year, an arrangement that gave Herod reason to hope for Cleopatra's downfall.

Antony did not stop at Judea and gave Cleopatra territories that had once been Ptolemaic but in recent years belonged to the Seleukid Empire. As a descendant of the fallen Seleukid Empire, Cleopatra believed that she had a legitimate claim to these lands, but only Antony had the power to give them to her. Cleopatra also added parts of the Syrian interior, Apameia, Chalkis, and Ituraia, parts of Crete, and a strategic coastal section of Nabatean Arabia to her empire.

There were no periods of significant civil unrest during Cleopatra's reign and no real disruption to the collection of taxes. Despite the fact that the Nile failed to flood in the years 42 and 41 BCE, a major agricultural disaster, Cleopatra managed to improve and expand agricultural production, leaving large surplus stores of grain and other foodstuffs on her death.

Yet it is important to acknowledge Cleopatra for what she was: an absolute monarch who ruled her people as a dictator. Cleopatra's incredible wealth and power were only sustainable through the subjugation of vast numbers of the Egyptian population. While it is true that the economic gap between middle-class Greeks and lower-class Egyptians lessened during Cleopatra's reign, this shift was accidental rather than by design. Overall, wealthy Greeks found their status diminished by currency debasement, foreign competition, and loss of territory while native Egyptians carried on much as before.

When Antony expanded the Ptolemaic Empire's territory in 37 BCE, Cleopatra found new streams of revenue. Collecting rental fees for Judean land from King Herod and exporting Egyptian products—such as linen, grain, and oil—Cleopatra managed to fill her treasury. Egypt's new riches were not spread among the kingdom's poorest citizens; instead, Cleopatra used them to fund Antony's disastrous Parthian campaign.

Chapter Seven

Antony and Cleopatra Reunited

*"Kingdoms are clay: our dungy earth alike
Feeds beast as man."*

—William Shakespeare, *Antony and Cleopatra*

The long-anticipated Parthian campaign set forth in the spring of 36 BCE. Not only did Cleopatra offer huge financial support to Antony's campaign, but she also joined him on his expedition as far as the Euphrates. Almost 50 years of ill feeling between the Parthians and Romans was finally supposed to end, and Caesar's dream of absorbing the Parthian Empire into the Roman Empire was to be realized.

From the Euphrates River, Cleopatra toured her new territories. In ancient times, it was imperative that new ruling powers visited their new lands so that the people could see their new leader and recognize the authority of their likeness, even when they ruled from far away. Cleopatra toured through Apameia in Syria, moving south through Damascus and visiting King Herod in Judea. After the tour, Cleopatra again receded from public view into her palace at Alexandria, as she was pregnant with her fourth child. Cleopatra named her third child Ptolemy Philadelphus, a reference to King Ptolemy II Philadelphus who ruled the Ptolemaic Kingdom at its most expansive.

While Cleopatra went through pregnancy, childbirth, and new motherhood again, Antony led a disastrous campaign. The Romans knew that any expedition into Parthian territory would be an incredibly long and complicated affair, yet Antony claimed to be able to win the war in one year. Antony had already proven himself as a gifted military tactician but realized by autumn 35 BCE that his campaign was doomed to fail.

Antony lost almost half his men, more than 24,000 soldiers, due to severe winter weather and disease. Antony had intended to set up winter quarters in Armenia, from which he could launch a strategic attack on Parthia in the spring. But the Armenian king, Artavasdes II, had deserted Antony at the crucial moment and forced him into retreat. By December, the Armenians had forced Antony into Ptolemaic territory where he waited, his army suffering from inadequate clothing and food until Cleopatra brought supplies.

News of Antony's humiliating defeat, one that did not even have a courageous battle at its center, reached Rome where the people met it with disgust. Antony's reputation back in Italy went into freefall, and the Roman people blamed Cleopatra for his Parthian failure. While Antony hid out at Cleopatra's palace in Alexandria, Octavian was free to take complete control of Antony's public image. A propaganda campaign ensued where Octavian deftly humiliated Antony and demonized Cleopatra.

Antony's treatment of his wife, Octavia, did not help his reputation. On hearing about the dire circumstances her husband and his army found themselves in, Octavia sent word that she was en route to Athens with supplies and extra troops in December 35 BCE. Cleopatra finally had Antony back in her life and did not want to relinquish her control on him to his wife. Perhaps Cleopatra convinced Antony to reject Octavia's offer of support, or perhaps Antony himself had no desire to see his wife; either way, Antony sent word to Octavia forbidding her from journeying east of Athens.

It was reasonable for Antony to want to keep Octavia safely in Rome as east of Athens was essentially an active war zone. But his relationship with Cleopatra complicated matters and on Octavia's return to Rome she took on the role of wronged victim. The people of Rome loved Octavia and recognized her as a morally astute member of the ruling class. By comparison, Romans saw Cleopatra as a foreign threat, a morally corrupt and lascivious seductress whose relationship with Antony could only spell disaster for Rome.

Next Antony took the foolish step of celebrating a triumph in Alexandria. The esteemed triumph celebration centered on the procession of a victorious Roman general to the Temple of Jupiter in Rome. In Alexandria, the event was a flop. Back in Rome, the people were aghast that Antony had defaced the ancient rites of Rome by acting them out for the Egyptians. Again, Cleopatra was to blame.

Soon after, Cleopatra orchestrated the Donations of Alexandria. The Donations are a startling example of Cleopatra's taste for theatricality and the emphasis she placed on her Hellenized origins. In an elaborate ceremony steeped in sacred Ptolemaic ritual, Cleopatra officially received the territories promised to her in 36 BCE and in return gave Antony extensive estates in Egypt.

Cleopatra, Antony, and Cleopatra's four children sat on golden thrones throughout the ceremony. Cleopatra, again dressed as Isis, took the titles Queen of Kings and Queen of Egypt, Libya, Cyprus, and Koile Syria. Cleopatra's eldest son, Caesarion, took the title King of Kings and joint ruler of Cleopatra's kingdoms. Alexander Helios, now six years old, also received the title King of Kings and was designated ruler of Armenia, Media and, ambitiously, Parthia. Cleopatra's last child, Ptolemy Philadelphus, also received the title King of Kings and, at just two years old, was given Syria, Kilikia, and all of Asia Minor.

Antony was a joint triumvirate of Rome with Octavian (Lepidus had been removed from the equation long ago) and so, in theory, had the power to gift these territories to Egypt. However, Antony's actions stripped Rome of its hard-won territory east of Asia Minor, and Octavian did not intend to let it go without a fight.

Chapter Eight

Propaganda Wars

*"Now from high heaven a new generation comes down.
Yet do thou at that boy's birth,
In whom the iron race shall begin to cease,
And the golden to arise over all the world."*

—Virgil, Fourth Eclogue

The Donations of Alexandria is just one example of the way Cleopatra sought to elevate herself in the eyes of her people to the status of more than human. Cleopatra had long drawn parallels between herself and the popular divinity, Isis.

Isis was the goddess of agriculture and the harvest and associated with marriage and maternity. A single mother of four children, Cleopatra had shaped her life in Isis' image. In Egyptian mythology, the god Horus fathered Isis' children. Horus was closely associated with Dionysus, the Greek god Antony frequently likened himself to. As the new Isis, Cleopatra took on the traditionally accepted appearance of Isis whenever she appeared in public and had coins minted showing this likeness. Following the Donations, Antony issued coins showing himself dressed as Dionysus and the couple had statues of themselves in their divine guises installed on the Acropolis in Athens.

In an attempt to counteract Octavian's barrage of propaganda that went as far as to suggest that Antony intended to bestow the city of Rome upon Cleopatra, Antony and Cleopatra promoted the idea that they were entering a new golden age. Tapping into ancient prophecies that said the world was soon to enter a new age of happiness and prosperity, Antony and Cleopatra used their child, Alexander Helios, to announce that the era had arrived.

In a poem written by Virgil in the year 40 BCE, Virgil predicts that the birth of a divine boy would signal the beginning of the new golden age. Despite the fact that Virgil had the union of Antony and Octavia in mind when he wrote the poem, Antony and Cleopatra insisted that this child was their son, Alexander Helios.

The Mediterranean east was completely polarized with Antony and Cleopatra on one side and Octavian and Octavia on the other; both sides promising a beautiful new golden age in which the various peoples of the east would be merged into one happy, peaceful family. On the floor of the Senate in Rome, defenders of Antony and Octavian fought out their rivalry with the argument essentially boiling down to who was the true and rightful heir of Caesar.

Octavian claimed that as the older adopted son of Caesar, he was the rightful heir, but Antony stood by Cleopatra, claiming that she was the mother of the only known child of Julius Caesar. Octavian argued that Antony had acted illegally in his arrest of Artavasdes II of Armenia, the king that had betrayed Antony during his

Parthian campaign of 35 BCE. Octavian also accused Antony of marrying Cleopatra, a personal slight on Octavian's family, a charge that may or may not have been true. In retaliation, Antony claimed that Octavian had illegally deposed Lepidus, the third member of the triumvirate, and that he had stolen Lepidus' troops.

The propaganda war that began in 34 BCE reached a fever pitch around 32 BCE. The most salacious and damaging rumors were not directed at either of the Roman triumvirates but at Cleopatra. Anecdotes and hearsay concerning Cleopatra's insatiable sexual appetite and proficiency as a sorceress titillated the people of Rome and later made their way into famous Roman writers' accounts of her life. The poet Lucan called Cleopatra "the shame of Egypt, the lascivious fury who was to become the bane of Rome." Likening Cleopatra to the ancient Greek figure of Medea, rather than the goddess Isis, the people of Rome saw the Egyptian queen as a monstrous creature of mythology; a drunken disgrace who resorted to prostitution and witchcraft to achieve her ends.

The Romans had long criticized Cleopatra for her excessive lifestyle. It was said that the queen could spend 2.5 million drachmas on one banquet, a staggering sum. Romans saw the extravagance of Cleopatra's lifestyle as distasteful and viewed Antony's involvement in them as a debasement of his character. Now, Romans added the charge of theft to their long list of grievances against Cleopatra. One Roman official accused Antony of removing the Library of Pergamon and giving its contents to Cleopatra to add to the collection at the Library of Alexandria. This story was not true, but that didn't stop the Roman public from believing it. Octavian also accused Antony of stealing sculptures to give to Cleopatra; Myron's Apollo was supposedly removed from Ephesus, and his Zeus, Athena, and Herakles were removed from Samos.

Public opinion of Antony in Rome was poor, but people reserved their ire almost exclusively for Cleopatra. When Antony was directly mentioned, it was to say that he had been bewitched by Cleopatra, that he had lost his powers of judgment and any mistakes he made were not truly his own. Slanderers criticized people publicly using graffiti or memorized and repeated poems. A popular poem written by Octavian some years earlier made fun of Antony's affair with Anatolian princess Glaphyra, and his wife, Fulvia's, reaction.

When the triumvirate expired at the end of 33 BCE, it was not renewed, and a war that would decide the fate of the ancient world was inevitable.

Chapter Nine

A War to End All Wars

"I shall be a good politician. Even if it kills me. Or if it kills anyone else, for that matter."

—Mark Antony

The final break between Antony and Octavian came in January 32 BCE when two consuls, sympathetic to Antony's cause, left the Senate with 300 senators and joined Antony in the east. Antony now set up a Senate of his own, and Cleopatra became an essential part of Antony's survival. Antony summoned his allied kings, and the couple traveled to Ephesus to pull together a naval force of 800 ships, including 200 of Cleopatra's.

Perhaps recognizing that Antony needed her more than ever, Cleopatra told Antony to divorce Octavia at this time. Antony duly sent an official notice of divorce to Octavia, a bold move that infuriated Octavian. Octavian seized Antony's will, something that could only have been achieved illegally, and used this document to decisively turn the people of Rome against Antony.

In a public reading, Octavian shared snippets from Antony's will that stated that Caesarion was the rightful heir of Caesar, that Antony wished to be buried in Egypt in Cleopatra's tomb, and that Antony planned to transfer the capital of the Roman Republic to Alexandria. It is unclear whether this will was legitimate or a forgery but either way, Octavian's public reading had the desired effect. Rome would not rest until it had destroyed Antony and his evil Cleopatra.

Both sides now focused on gathering the largest army they possibly could. Cleopatra and Antony's 800 ships were accompanied by more than 100,000 troops and the support of 11 independent allied kings. By contrast, Octavian had just 200 ships and 80,000 soldiers. However, a large proportion of Cleopatra and Antony's drafted troops were untrained merchants, while the entirety of Octavian's army was military trained.

By the spring of 31 BCE, Antony and Cleopatra stationed their cast naval force at Aktion in the Ambracian Gulf of northwest Greece. Cleopatra knew that she had to maintain control of the seas on the Greek coast if she was to defend Egypt from Octavian's forces. Octavian moved his troops to the island of Kerkyra (now Corfu) and tried to disrupt the movement of supplies to Antony and Cleopatra's army.

Throughout the summer, the two armies were involved in minor engagements that generally ended in victory for Octavian. Perhaps realizing that they had backed the wrong horse, some allied kings, supposedly loyal to Antony and Cleopatra, changed sides. Fearing for her kingdom's security, Cleopatra wanted to return to Egypt leaving only a skeleton force in place. Antony's military generals wanted to withdraw into mainland Greece and continue the battle on land, but Cleopatra knew that she could only keep Egypt safe by destroying Octavian's navy.

On September 2, 31 BCE, Antony and Cleopatra orchestrated a decisive naval engagement known as the Battle of Actium. Cleopatra sailed at the helm of the *Antonias*, leading a detachment of 60 ships at the mouth of the Ambracian Gulf. Cleopatra's fleet was placed at the rear of the main forces, Antony's attempt to either protect her or marginalize her in the battle. In the midst of the battle, realizing that she was in no position to defend Egypt and sensing the battle was already lost, Cleopatra maneuvered her ships through the fighting and headed south for the Peloponnese. Antony ordered his ship to follow his queen and boarded the *Antonias* himself.

It took three days for Antony and Cleopatra to reach the port of Tainaron at the southern point of Peloponnese, by which time the Battle of Actium had been lost. News spread that Antony and Cleopatra had fled the battle, and a huge number of senior officers and ordinary men defected, pledging an allegiance to Octavian to save themselves. By the morning of the 3rd of September, Octavian had taken possession of the Greek mainland and established himself in Athens, a city historically allied with Cleopatra.

Antony and Cleopatra traveled from Tainaron into Egypt. Antony went to Cyrene, believing that he might yet mobilize a land force capable of beating Octavian, and Cleopatra returned to Alexandria. Cleopatra tried desperately to win new allies to help her fight back against Octavian's advance on Egypt to no avail. All of the allied kings pledged allegiance to Octavian, even Herod. Now Cleopatra and Antony had not a single ally between Greece and Egypt.

Chapter Ten

The Last Pharaoh of Egypt

"I will not be led in triumph."

—Cleopatra VII

After the defeat of her navy at the Battle of Actium and the subsequent desertion of all of her allies, Cleopatra revealed the true strength of her character. While Antony retreated from society and lived alone in a beach hut on the island of Pharos, Cleopatra made increasingly desperate attempts to secure her kingdom. Antony was suicidal and living as a hermit, but his very existence made a peaceful resolution between Cleopatra and Octavian impossible.

The only way for Cleopatra to save Egypt would be to withdraw from it. Cleopatra tried to clear the way for her son, Caesarion, to take over the rule of Egypt in the hope that this would deflect much of the Roman hostility directed at her. Around August 31 BCE, Cleopatra left Egypt perhaps intending to live out her days in India. Cleopatra hatched a plan, independent of Antony, to take her remaining fleet of ships from the Mediterranean, somehow drag them across the isthmus and re-launch them on the Red Sea. From there, Cleopatra could start a new life. But before Cleopatra could carry out this plan,

King Malchos, her sworn enemy, burned her entire fleet and she was forced to stay in Egypt.

Antony and Cleopatra had no choice but to try to negotiate with Octavian. It was clear that Octavian held all of the power. Negotiations went on for several months but led nowhere. Aware that Antony had become an ineffective liability, Cleopatra contacted Octavian secretly and asked for permission to hand Egypt over to her children. To sweeten the deal, Cleopatra sent Octavian a golden scepter, crown, and throne and promised huge sums of money should he agree to her terms. Cleopatra's focus was the protection of Egypt, whether she was queen or not, but the fact that her eldest son was Octavian's rival complicated matters. While Octavian entered into a dialogue with Cleopatra, he ignored any message sent by Antony. When both Antony and Cleopatra began to threaten suicide, vowing to destroy their treasure and wealth in the process, Octavian was forced to act.

In early 30 BCE, Octavian moved his forces south of Athens and, with the help of King Herod, reached the Egyptian frontier at Pelousion with a fully supplied and well-trained army. Pelousion fell easily, and Octavian's army proceeded to Alexandria. Antony sprung back into action, leading an army to meet Octavian's troops near the Hippodrome. In this engagement, Antony was successful, but when he sent out a fleet the next day it deserted him for Octavian, as did a cavalry he sent out soon after.

Throughout these engagements, Cleopatra remained in Alexandria, hidden in her tomb. Romantic retellings of what happened next focus on Antony and Cleopatra's suicide pact, suggesting that the pair committed suicide because they could not bear to be without each other. In reality, Cleopatra's motives at least may have been more strategic than romantic.

Cleopatra had word sent to Antony that she had committed suicide. Antony had threatened to commit suicide himself a number of times since the Battle of Actium and Cleopatra thought that if Antony thought she was dead, he would kill himself. She was right. On hearing news of Cleopatra's suicide, Antony turned his sword on himself and stabbed himself in the stomach. Antony had chosen a painful and slow method of suicide and lived for a number of hours.

In that time, Cleopatra ordered that his body be brought to her at her tomb. Antony finally died in Cleopatra's arms, aged 53. Cleopatra gained Octavian's permission to embalm Antony. Whether Cleopatra embalmed Antony herself is unclear, it is possible the queen was able to perform this task and had his body buried in her tomb, as he requested in his will.

Even now, Cleopatra's focus was on her kingdom. Octavian desperately wanted to get his hands on Egypt's great wealth and could have taken Cleopatra's kingdom and left her alive. However, Cleopatra would have rather died than lived to see her kingdom taken by Rome. Cleopatra was a major religious figure, the mother of Caesar's only blood child, and she and her children were the only surviving members of the ancient Ptolemaic dynasty. To kill her would cause all of Egypt to rebel, but to let her live would leave Octavian vulnerable to violent uprisings in her name.

Octavian addressed the people of Alexandria, insisting he sought reconciliation between Egypt and Rome and took up quarters in the palace. It was only a matter of time before Octavian would lead a triumph back in Rome. Having borne witness to the humiliating Markh Caesar forced her sister, Arsinoe, to endure in 46 BCE, Cleopatra decided that suicide was her only option. She would not be led in triumph, no matter what the cost.

On August 10, 30 BCE, Cleopatra and two of her closest advisors and ladies in waiting enjoyed an elaborate meal in her tomb. In the account of what happened next most widely accepted by historians, Cleopatra had a message sent to Octavian, requesting that she be buried in her tomb alongside Antony. On receiving the message, Octavian knew what Cleopatra was orchestrating. Cleopatra must have consumed the poison first, as when Octavian reached the tomb she was already dead. Cleopatra's ladies in waiting had carefully laid out her body in full royal regalia and now lay, almost dead themselves. Cleopatra was 39 years old.

One of Cleopatra's last actions was to secure safe passage for Caesarion to travel to Upper Egypt where he would wait for Octavian's next move. It was entirely possible that although Rome would officially take control of Egypt, Octavian would install Caesarion as its rightful king. Soon after Cleopatra's death, Caesarion received word that he was to return to Alexandria where Octavian would formally announce him as king. Octavian, however, sent an assassin to kill Caesarion while he was still on the road. Octavian picked off other claimants to the Egypt throne one by one, including Antony's eldest son, Antyllus. On August 29, 30 BCE, the ruling Ptolemaic dynasty officially ended.

Conclusion

When Octavian eliminated claimants to the Egyptian throne after Cleopatra's death, he spared the children. Cleopatra's twins, Alexander Helios and Cleopatra Selene, and their younger brother, Ptolemy Philadelphus were sent to Rome where Octavia raised them. Both Alexander and Ptolemy died during childhood, but it's not clear whether or not their deaths were suspicious. Cleopatra Selene lived into adulthood and was married to another royal refugee, Juba II, son of Numidian king Juba I. Octavian gave Cleopatra and Juba the kingdom of Mauretania in northwest Africa where the young couple cultivated a Ptolemaic court, in culture if not in name.

Cleopatra's legacy lived on throughout Octavian's reign, despite his best efforts to suppress it. In the year 27 BCE, Octavian became Emperor Augustus. By this time, Octavian had already divided the Ptolemaic Empire, absorbing certain territories into the Roman Republic and bestowing others upon the allied kings who had betrayed Antony and Cleopatra. Octavian never returned to Egypt, perhaps haunted by what had happened there.

The Roman world Octavian created as emperor bore many resemblances to the Cleopatra's Egypt. Octavian built temples, mausoleums, and obelisks that mimicked those found in Alexandria, and Roman sculpture, painting, and mosaic work took on an Egyptian style that lasted for centuries.

In contemporary times, Cleopatra is a figure of pop culture more than she is a figure of world history. Inspired by Renaissance drama and Romantic poets, filmmakers, artists, and advertising executives have created their own versions of Cleopatra's life story and image. As a constructed icon of cultural history—think Cleopatra, think Elizabeth Taylor—Cleopatra's history is reduced to myth.

Yet up to her last moment on this earth, Cleopatra was in control of her image, her fate, and her legacy. After her death, her story ended up in Roman hands, but even the most gifted Roman rhetorician could not erase the memory of the audacious queen, who captivated not one but two of the greatest Roman men of her time and who left this world unconquered.

Made in the USA
San Bernardino, CA
27 February 2018